THE VESPERS OF PENTECOST

(With the "Kneeling" Prayers)

In Large Print Format

The Vespers of Pentecost
(with the 'Kneeling Prayers')

Priest   Blessed is our God, always, now and ever and unto ages of ages.

Choir   (Tone 6) Amen. O Heavenly King, the Comforter, the Spirit of Truth, who art everywhere and fillest all things, treasury of blessings and giver of life, come and abide in us and cleanse us from every impurity, and save our souls, O good one.

Reader   Holy God, Holy Mighty, Holy Immortal, have mercy on us (3x)

Glory to the Father and to the Son and to the Holy Spirit, now and ever and unto ages of ages. Amen.

Most Holy Trinity have mercy on us, Lord cleanse us from our sins, Master pardon our transgressions, Holy One, visit and heal our infirmities for Thy Name's sake.

Lord have mercy, Lord have mercy, Lord have mercy.

Glory to the Father and to the Son and to the Holy Spirit, now and ever and unto ages of ages. Amen.

Our Father, who art in heaven, hallowed be Thy name. Thy kingdom come, Thy will be done on earth as it is in heaven. Give us this day our daily bread and forgive us our trespasses as we forgive those who trespass against us. And lead us not into temptation but deliver us from evil.

Priest   For Thine is the Kingdom, and the power and the glory, now and ever and unto ages of ages.

Reader   Amen. Lord have mercy (12x)

Glory to the Father and to the Son and to the Holy Spirit, now and ever and unto ages of ages. Amen.

Come, let us worship God, our King! Come, let us worship and fall down before Christ our King and our God! Come, let us worship and fall down before Christ Himself, our King and our God!

PSALM 104

Bless the Lord, O my soul! O Lord my God, thou art very great! Thou art clothed with honor and majesty, who coverest thyself with light as with a garment, who hast stretched out the heavens like a tent, who hast laid the beams of thy chambers on the waters, who makest the clouds thy chariot, who ridest on the wings of the wind, who makest the winds thy messengers, fire and flame thy ministers.

Thou didst set the earth on its foundations, so that it should never be shaken. Thou didst cover it with the deep as with a garment; the waters stood above the mountains. At thy rebuke they fled; at the sound of thy thunder they took to flight.

The mountains rose, the valleys sank down to the place which thou didst appoint for them. Thou didst set a bound which they should not pass, so that they might not again cover the earth.

Thou makest springs gush forth in the valleys; they flow between the hills; they give drink to every beast of the field; the wild asses quench their thirst.

By them the birds of the air have their habitation; they sing among the branches. From thy lofty abode thou waterest the mountains; the earth is satisfied with the fruit of thy work.

Thou dost cause the grass to grow for the cattle, and plants for man to cultivate, that he may bring forth food from the earth and wine to gladden the heart of man, oil to make his face shine, and bread to strengthen man's heart.

The trees of the Lord are watered abundantly, the cedars of Lebanon which he planted. In them the birds build their nests; the stork has her home in the fir trees. The high mountains are for the wild goats; the rocks are a refuge for the badgers.

Thou hast made the moon to mark the seasons; the sun knows it's time for setting. Thou makest darkness, and it is night, when all the beasts of the forest creep forth.
The young lions roar for their prey, seeking their food from God.

When the sun rises, they get them away and lie down in their dens. Man goes forth to his work and to his labor until the evening. O Lord, how manifold are thy works! In wisdom hast thou made them all; the earth is full of thy creatures.

Yonder is the sea, great and wide, which teems with things innumerable, living things both small and great. There go the ships and Leviathan which thou didst form to sport in it. These all look to thee, to give them their food in due season.

When thou givest to them, they gather it up; when thou openest thy hand, they are filled with good things. When thou hidest thy face, they are dismayed; when thou takest away their breath, they die and return to their dust. When thou sendest forth thy Spirit, they are created; and Thou renewest the face of the ground.

May the glory of the Lord endure forever, may the Lord rejoice in His works, who looks on the earth and it trembles, who touches the mountains, and they smoke! I will sing to the Lord as long as I live; I will sing praise to my God while I have being.

May my meditation be pleasing to Him, for I rejoice in the Lord. Let sinners be consumed from the earth and let the wicked be no more! Bless the Lord, O my soul! The sun knows it's time for setting. Thou makest darkness and it is night. O Lord, how manifold are Thy works! In wisdom hast Thou made them all!

Glory to the Father, and to the Son, and to the Holy Spirit, now and ever, and unto ages of ages.

Amen. Alleluia, Alleluia, Alleluia, Glory to Thee, O God. (3x)

The Great Litany

Priest   In peace, let us pray to the Lord

Choir   Lord, have mercy

For the peace from above and for the salvation of our souls, let us pray to the Lord.

For the peace of the whole world, for the welfare of the holy churches of God, and for the union of all, let us pray to the Lord.

For this holy house and for those who enter with faith, reverence, and the fear of God, let us pray to the Lord.

For His Beatitude, Our Metropolitan __________ , and for His (Eminence, Grace) our (Archbishop, Bishop) __________ for the honorable priesthood, the deaconate in Christ, for all the clergy and the people, let us pray to the Lord.

For the President of our country, for all civil authorities, and for our armed forces everywhere, let us pray to the Lord.

For this city, for every city and country, and for the faithful dwelling in them, let us pray to the Lord.

For seasonable weather, for abundance of the fruits of the earth, and for peaceful times, let us pray to the Lord.

For travelers by land, by sea, and by air; for the sick and the suffering; for captives and their salvation, let us pray to the Lord.

For the people here present who await the grace of the Holy Spirit, let us pray to the Lord.

For those that bow their hearts and their knees before the Lord, let us pray to the Lord

That He may strengthen us so that we may fulfill those things that are well- pleasing to Him, let us pray to the Lord.

That He may send down the riches of His mercy upon us, let us pray to the Lord.

That He may accept the bending of our knees as incense before Him, let us pray to the Lord.

For those that are in need of His help, let us pray to the Lord.

For our deliverance from all affliction, wrath, danger, and necessity, let us pray to the Lord.

Help us, save us, have mercy on us, and keep us, O God, by Thy grace.

Commemorating our most holy, most pure, most blessed and glorious Lady Theotokos and Ever-virgin Mary, with all the saints, let us commend ourselves and each other, and all our life unto Christ our God.

Choir   To Thee, O Lord.

Priest   For unto Thee are due all glory, honor, and worship: to the Father, and to the Son, and to the Holy Spirit, now and ever and unto ages of ages.

Choir   Amen

The priest enters the Sanctuary through the south deacon's doors. Having venerated the alter table, he takes the censer and begins the customary censing during "Lord I Call."

Lord I Call (Tone 4)

Choir   Lord, I call upon Thee, hear me. Hear me, O Lord. Lord, I call upon Thee, hear me. Receive the voice of my prayer when I call upon Thee. Hear me, O Lord.

Let my prayer arise in Thy sight as incense and let the lifting up of my hands be an evening sacrifice. Hear me, O Lord.

Reader   *If Thou, O Lord, shouldst mark iniquities, Lord, who could stand? But there is forgiveness with Thee.*

Choir   Today the nations have beheld wondrous things in the city of David when the Holy Spirit descended in fiery tongues as the Divine Luke records: a sound as of mighty rushing wind filled the house where the disciples of Christ were assembled. They began uttering strange doctrines in strange words, strange teachings of the Holy Trinity.

Reader *From the morning watch until night, from the morning watch let Israel hope in the Lord.*

Choir The Holy Spirit was, is, and ever shall be without beginning, without an end, forever united and numbered with the Father and the Son. He is Life, and life-creating, the Light, and the Giver of Light, Good in Himself, the Fountain of goodness, through whom the Father is known and the Son glorified. All acknowledge one Power, one Order, One worship of the Holy Trinity.

Reader *Praise the Lord, all nations; praise Him all peoples.*

Choir The Holy Spirit is Light and Life, the living Fountain of spiritual gifts: The Spirit of wisdom, the Spirit of understanding. He is good, upright, intelligent and ruling. He purifies us from our sins. The Spirit is the deifying God; fire proceeding from fire, Speaking, acting, distributing gifts. By the Spirit the prophets, divine apostles and martyrs were crowned. Strange is this report! Strange is this sight. Fire is divided for the granting of gifts.

Reader *Glory to the Father, and to the Son and to the Holy Spirit, now and ever and unto ages of ages. Amen.*

The Royal Doors are now opened, and te priest and serevers make the Entrance as the choir sings the Dogmatic (O Heavenly King).

Choir (Tone 6) O Heavenly King, / the Comforter, the Spirit of Truth, / who art everywhere and fillest all things, / treasury of blessings / and giver of life, / come and abide in us / and cleanse us from every impurity, // and save our souls, O good one.

Gladsome Light

Standing before the Royal Doors, the priest blesses the entrance saying:

Priest Blessed is the entrance of Thy saints, always, now and ever and unto ages of ages.

Then, while elevating the censer, he intones:

Priest Wisdom! Let us attend!

Choir: O gladsome light of the Holy Glory of the Immortal Father - heavenly, holy, blessed Jesus Christ! Now that we hve come to the setting of the sun and see the light of evening, we praise God: Father, Son and Holy Spirit. For meet it is at all times to worship Thee with voices of prise, O Son of God and Given of life. Therefore, all the world doth glorify thee.

The priest completes the Entrance by going to the High Place and facing the people, he intones:

The Great Prokeimenon

Priest Let us attend! Peace be to all! The Great Prokeimenon is in the 7th Tone: Who is so great a God as our God; Thou art the God who does wonders.

Choir Who is so great a God as our God; Thou art the God who does wonders.

Priest Thou hast made known Thy power among the peoples.

Choir Who is so great….

Priest And I said, now have I begun; this is the change of the right hand of the Most High.

Choir Who is so great…

Priest I remembered the works of the Lord; for from the beginning will I remember thy wonders.

Choir Who is so great…

Priest Who is so great a God as our God

Choir Thou art the God who does wonders.

It is customary for all (who are able) to kneel and remain so while the priest (also kneeling) reads the prayer in the open Royal Doors and facing the people. At the Litany, all may rise.

The First Prayer

Priest   Again and again, on bended knees, let us pray to the Lord

Choir   Lord, have mercy (3)

O Lord, who art immaculate, spotless, without beginning, invisible, incomprehensible, inscrutable, unchanging, unsurpassable, immeasurable, forbearing, who alone hast immortality, who dwellest in light unapproachable, who hast made heaven and earth and the sea, and all created things therein, who grantest unto all men their petitions before they ask, we pray Thee and beseech Thee, O Master, who lovest man, the Father of our Lord and God and Savior, Jesus Christ, who for us men and for our salvation came down from heaven, and was incarnate by the Holy Spirit and of Mary the Ever-virgin and most glorious Theotokos, who first did teach in words and afterwards did show by deeds, when He endured His saving Passion, who did give us,

Thy humble, and sinful, and unworthy servants, an example, whereby we should offer unto Thee prayers with the bending of the neck and the knees, both for our own sins and for the ignorance of the people; do Thou Thyself, who art great in mercy and lovest man, hear us in that day when we shall call upon Thee, and especially on this day of Pentecost, on which, after our Lord Jesus Christ had ascended into the heavens, and had sat down at the right hand of Thee, the God and Father,

He did send down the Holy Spirit upon His holy disciples and apostles, which did also rest upon each of them, and they were all filled with His inexhaustible grace, and they spake with other tongues of Thy greatness, and they prophesied.

Hearken, therefore, to us now who pray to Thee, and remember us, humble and condemned as we are, and turn again the captivity of our souls, Thou that hast Thine own compassion as intercessor for us. Receive us who fall down before Thee and cry, we have sinned. We have cleaved unto Thee from our birth, even from our mother's womb. Thou art our God, but since our days have passed in vanity, we have been stripped of Thine help we have been deprived of every defense.

But emboldened by Thy compassions, we call out, Remember not the sins of our youth and our ignorance and cleanse Thou us of our secret sins, cast us not away in time of old age; when our strength faileth, forsake us not. Before we return to the earth, make us worthy to turn again unto Thee, and attend to us in favor and grace.

Measure our transgressions according to Thy compassion, set the depth of Thy compassion against the multitude of our offenses. Look down from Thy holy heights, O Lord, upon Thy people here present who await of Thee rich mercy. Visit us in Thy goodness.

Deliver us from the power of the Devil. Make firm our lives with Thy holy and sacred laws. Entrust Thy people to a faithful guardian Angel. Gather us all into Thy kingdom. Grant pardon to those that hope in Thee. Forgive them and us our sins. Purify us by the operation of Thy Holy Spirit. Destroy the snares set for us by the enemy.

And then he adds this prayer:

Blessed art Thou, O Lord, Master Almighty, who hast lightened the day with the light of the sun, and hast illuminated the night with flashes of fire, who hast vouchsafed us to pass through the length of the day and to draw near to the beginning of the night, hearken to our prayer and to that of all Thy people, and having pardoned us all our voluntary and involuntary sins, receive our evening supplications, and send down the multitude of Thy mercies and compassions upon Thine inheritance.

Wall us in with Thy holy Angels. Arm us with the armor of Thy righteousness. Make a bulwark about us with Thy truth. Guard us with Thy power. Deliver us from every oppression and every plot of the adversary. Grant us also that the present evening with the coming night, and all the days of our life, may be perfect, holy, peaceful, sinless, without stumbling-blocks, without, fantasy, through the intercessions of the holy Theotokos and of all the Saints, who have in all ages been well-pleasing unto Thee.

Help us, save us, have mercy on us, raise us up, and keep us, O God, by Thy grace.

Choir   Lord have mercy.

Priest   Commemorating our most holy, most pure, most blessed and glorious Lady Theotokos and Ever-virgin Mary, with all the saints, let us commend ourselves and each other, and all our life unto Christ our God.

Choir   To Thee, O Lord.

Priest   For Thine it is to have mercy on us and to save us, O our God, and unto Thee do we send up glory, to the Father, and to the Son, and to the Holy Spirit, now and ever, and unto ages of ages.

Choir   Amen

The Augmented Litany

Priest   Let us say with all our soul and with all our mind, let us say.

Choir   Lord, have mercy.

O Lord almighty, the God of our fathers, we pray Thee, hearken and have mercy.

Choir   Lord, have mercy.

Priest   Have mercy on us, O God, according to Thy great goodness, we pray Thee, hearken and have mercy.

Choir   Lord, have mercy (3x)

Again we pray for His Beatitude, our Metropolitan __________ and His (Eminence, Grace), our (Archbishop, Bishop) ________, for priests, deacons, and all other clergy; and for all our brethren in Christ.

Again we pray for the President of our country, for all civil authorities, and for the armed forces.

Again we pray for the blessed and ever-memorable founders of this holy house; and for all of our fathers, mothers, brothers and sisters, the Orthodox departed this life before us, who here and in all the world lie asleep in the Lord.

Again we pray for mercy, life, peace, health, salvation, and visitation, pardon and remission of sins, for all the brethren of this holy house.

Again we pray for those who bring offerings and do good works in this holy and all-venerable house; for those who labor and those who sing; and for all people here present, who await Thy great and rich mercy.

For Thou art a merciful God, and lovest mankind, and unto Thee we ascribe glory: to the Father, and to the Son, and to the Holy Spirit, now and ever and unto ages of ages.

Choir   Amen

All kneel as before.

The Second Prayer

Priest   Again and again, on bended knees, let us pray to the Lord.

Choir   Lord, have mercy (3x)

Priest   O Lord Jesus Christ our God, who hast given Thy
peace to men, and being present still in this life, dost ever
grant the gift of the Holy Spirit to the faithful, as an
inheritance that cannot be taken away, Thou didst send
down today in manner most clear, this grace upon Thy holy
disciples and apostles, and didst open their lips with
tongues of fire.

Through them every race of man hath received, through
the hearing of the ear, the knowledge of God in our own
languages. We have been enlightened by the light of the
Spirit, and we have been freed from delusion as from
darkness, and through the distribution of the perceptible
tongues of fire, and the wondrous operation of the same, we
have been taught the faith that is in Thee, and we have been
illumined so as to confess Thee, with the Father and the Holy
Spirit, in one Godhead, and power, and authority.

For Thou art the brightness of the Father, the express
image, inalterable and immovable, of His essence and
nature, the fountain of wisdom and of grace. Open Thou the
lips of me a sinner and teach me how I ought and for what I
must pray. For Thou knowest the multitude of my sins, but
Thy tenderness shall overcome the enormity thereof. For, lo,
in fear I stand before Thee; into the sea of Thy mercy have I
cast the desperation of my soul.

Order my life, Thou that orderest all creation with Thy
word, and with the unutterable power of Thy wisdom, O
tranquil haven of the storm-tossed, and make known to me

the way wherein I should walk. Grant to my reasoning the Spirit of Thy wisdom and give the Spirit of understanding to my foolishness. Overshadow my deeds with the Spirit of Thy fear and renew a right Spirit in my inmost parts.

And with Thy guiding Spirit, establish my faltering mind, that being guided every day by Thy good Spirit toward what is useful, I may be vouchsafed to keep Thy commandments and always to remember Thy glorious coming-again, which shall search out our deeds. Despise me not, lest I be deceived by the corrupting pleasures of this world but enable me to yearn for the enjoyment of the treasures of that to come.

For Thou hast said, O Master, that whatsoever may be asked in Thy name, shall be freely received of Thy coeternal God and Father. I, a sinner, therefore, at the descent of Thy Holy Spirit, do supplicate Thy goodness, Do Thou render unto me whatsoever I have asked unto salvation. Yea, O Lord, the good and abundant Giver of every benefit, for Thou art He that granteth most abundantly that which we ask.

Thou art He that sinlessly became the compassionate, merciful partaker of our flesh; and to those that bend their knees before Thee, dost Thou graciously bend down and become the propitiation for our sins.

Grant then, Lord, Thy compassion to Thy people. Hearken to us from Thy holy heaven. Sanctify them by the power of Thy saving right hand. Shelter them with the shelter of Thy wings. Despise not the work of Thy hands. Against Thee alone do we sin, but Thee alone do we also adore.

We know not how to worship a strange god, nor how to stretch forth our hands to any other god, O Master. Forgive us our offenses and accept our prayers with the bending of our knees; extend to us all the hand of Thine aid and receive the prayer of all as an acceptable incense, rising before Thy blessed kingdom.

And then he adds this prayer:

O Lord, Lord, who deliverest us from every arrow that flieth by day, deliver us also from everything that walketh about in the darkness. Accept the lifting up of our hands as an evening sacrifice. Vouchsafe us also to pass, without reproach the course of the night untempted of evil things and redeem us from every disturbance and dread that cometh to us from the devil.

Grant unto our souls contrition and unto our thoughts care concerning the trial of Thy fearful and righteous judgment. Nail our flesh to the fear of Thee and mortify our earthly members, that even in the quietness of sleep we may be illumined by the contemplation of Thy Judgments. Withdraw from us every unseemly fantasy and injurious desire. Raise us up at the time of prayer confirmed in the faith and progressing in Thy commandments.

Help us, save us, have mercy on us, raise us up, and keep us, O God, by Thy grace.

Choir   Lord, have mercy.

Priest   Commemorating our most holy, most pure, most blessed and glorious Lady Theotokos and Ever-virgin Mary, with all the saints, let us commend ourselves and each other, and all our life unto Christ our God.

Choir　To Thee, O Lord

Priest　Through the favor and grace of Thine only-begotten Son, with whom Thou art blessed, together with Thine all holy, and good, and life-creating Spirit, now and ever, and unto ages of ages.

Choir　Amen

Reader　Vouchsafe, O Lord, to keep us this night without sin. Blessed art Thou, O Lord, the God of our fathers, and praised and glorified is Thy name forever. Amen. Let Thy mercy be upon us, O Lord, even as we have set our hope on Thee. Blessed art Thou, O Lord; teach me Thy statutes. Blessed art Thou, O Master; make me to understand Thy commandments. Blessed art Thou, O Holy One; enlighten me with Thy precepts. Thy mercy, O Lord, endureth forever: O despise not the works of Thy hands. To Thee belongeth worship, to Thee belongeth praise, to Thee belongeth glory, to the Father, and to the Son, and to the Holy Spirit, now and ever, and unto ages of ages. Amen.

The Third Prayer

Once again, all kneel.

Priest　Again and again, on bended knees, let us pray to the Lord.

Choir　Lord, have mercy (3x)

Priest   O ever-flowing Fountain of life and light, creative power coeternal with the Father, who hast most excellently fulfilled the whole dispensation of the, salvation of mankind, Christ our God, who didst burst the indestructible bonds of death and the bolts of Hell, and hast trampled down the multitude of evil spirits; who didst offer Thyself as a blameless victim, giving Thine immaculate body as a sacrifice, unblemished and inviolate of all sin, and through that dread and indescribable act of sacrifice, bestowed eternal life upon us; who didst descend into Hell and break down its eternal bars, showing forth the way up to those who sat in the lower world;

who with allurements of divine wisdom, didst entice the author of evil, the dragon of the abyss, and with cords of gloom didst bind him in Hell and in unquenchable fire, and Thou didst confine him in outer darkness by Thine infinite might, Thou who art the greatly glorified wisdom of the Father, didst manifest Thyself as a great Helper to the oppressed, and didst enlighten those that sat in darkness and in the shadow of death, Thou Lord of eternal glory and beloved Son of the Father most high, Light everlasting of Light everlasting, Sun of righteousness:

Hearken to us who pray unto Thee, and give rest to the souls of Thy servants, our fathers and brethren, who have fallen asleep before us, and our other kinsmen after the flesh, and all Thine own who are in the faith, of whom we now make memorial, for in Thee is the power over all, and in Thine hand Thou holdest all the ends of the earth. Almighty Master, God of the fathers and Lord of mercies,

Maker of the race of mortals and immortals, and of every nature of man, of that which is brought together and again put asunder, of life and of the end of life, of sojourning here and of translation there, who dost measure the years of life and set the times of death, who bringest down to Hell and raisest up, binding in infirmity and releasing unto power, dispensing present things according to need, and ordering those to come as is expedient, quickening with the hope of resurrection those that are smitten with the sting of death.

Thyself, O Master of all, God our Savior, the hope of all the ends of the earth and of those that are far off upon the sea, who on this last and great and saving day of Pentecost, didst show forth to us the mystery of the Holy Trinity, consubstantial and coeternal, undivided and unmingled, and didst pour out the descent and presence of Thy holy and life-creating Spirit in the form of tongues of fire, upon Thy holy Apostles, appointing them to be the Evangelists of our pious faith, and showing them to be confessors and preachers of the true theology;

who also on this all-perfect and saving feast, dost deign to receive oblations and supplications for those bound in Hell, and grantest unto us the great hope that respite and comfort will be sent down from Thee to the departed from the grief that doth bind them.

Hearken to us Thy humble and piteous ones who pray and give rest to the souls of Thy servants who have fallen asleep before us, in a place of light, in a place of refreshment, in a place of repose, whence all sickness, sorrow, and sighing are fled away; and do Thou place their souls in the tabernacles of the righteous and make them worthy of peace and repose.

For the dead praise Thee not, neither do those in Hell dare to offer Thee confession, but we, the living, bless Thee, and supplicate Thee, and offer them propitiatory prayers and sacrifices for their souls.

And then he adds this prayer:

O God, who art great and eternal holy and lovest mankind, who hast vouchsafed us also to stand before Thine unapproachable glory, that we may hymn and praise Thy wonders, cleanse us Thine unworthy servants, and grant grace that with contrite heart and without presumption, we may offer Thee the thrice-holy glorification and thanksgiving for Thy great gifts, which Thou hast granted and dost ever grant us.

Remember, O Lord, our infirmities and destroy us not for our transgressions, but be merciful to our humility that fleeing from the darkness of sin we may walk in the day of righteousness, and, clothed with the armor of light, may persevere unassailed from every attack of the Evil One, so that with boldness we may glorify Thee in all things, the only true God and Lover of mankind.

For Thine in truth is the mystery, O Master and Maker of both the temporary dissolution of creatures and their restoration thereafter, and of eternal rest. We confess Thy grace in all things, in our coming into this world, and in our going therefrom, which things faith pledge unto us, through Thine unfailing promise, our hopes of the resurrection and of life incorruptible, which we shall receive hereafter at Thy Second Coming.

For Thou art both the Author of our resurrection and the impartial Judge of those that have lived, and the Lover of man, and the Master and Lord of recompense, who didst partake with us, on equal terms, of flesh and blood, through Thine extreme condescension, and of our irreproachable passions, wherein Thou didst willingly submit to temptation, since Thou dost possess tenderness and compassion, and Thyself, having suffered temptation, art become for us who are tempted, the Helper which Thou Thyself hadst promised to be, and therefore Thou hast led us to Thy passionlessness.

Accept, therefore, O Master, our prayers and supplications, and give rest to all the fathers and mothers, and children, and brothers and sisters of each of us, and to any others of our kindred and of our people, and to every soul that hath gone to rest before in the hope of resurrection unto life eternal.

Set their spirits and their names in the book of life, in the bosom of Abraham, Isaac and Jacob, in the land of the living, in the kingdom of heaven, in a Paradise of bliss, leading all, by Thy radiant Angels, into Thy holy abode, raising up also with Thee our bodies in the day which hast been appointed according to Thy holy and unfailing promise.

There is, therefore, O Lord, no death unto Thy servants, when we go forth from the body and come unto Thee, our God, but a change from things most sorrowful unto things most beneficent and most sweet, and rest and joy. And, though we have sinned against Thee, be gracious unto us and unto them, for none is pure of stain in Thy sight, though his life be but for one day, except Thou alone, who didst reveal Thyself sinless on the earth, O Lord Jesus Christ, of whom we all hope to obtain mercy and the forgiveness of sins.

Do Thou, therefore, as the good God who lovest man, remit, forgive, pardon them and us of our offenses, voluntary and involuntary, those done with knowledge or in ignorance, those manifest or unnoticed, those of deed, of thought, of word, those of all our acts and movements; and to those who have been taken from us give freedom and respite, and bless us who are here present, granting a good and peaceful ending to us and to all Thy people, and open to us Thy tender mercies and Thy love of man at Thy dread and fearful coming again, and make us worthy of Thy kingdom.

And then he adds this prayer:

O great and most high God, who alone hast immortality, and dwellest in light unapproachable, who hast fashioned all creation in wisdom, who hast divided the light from the darkness and hast set the sun to rule the day and the moon and stars to rule the night, who hast also vouchsafed unto us sinners at this present hour to come before Thy presence with confession and to present unto Thee our evening prayer, do Thou Thyself, O Lord, Lover of man, direct our prayer as incense before Thee, and accept it for a sweet spiritual fragrance, and grant that our present evening and coming night be peaceful.

Clothe us with the armor of light. Deliver us from the fear of night, and from everything that walketh in darkness, and grant that the sleep that Thou hast given for the repose of our infirmity may be free from every fantasy of the Devil. Yea, O Master of all, Leader of the good, may we, being moved to compunction upon our beds, remember Thy name in the night.

And, enlightened by the exercise of Thy commandments, may we rise up in joyfulness of soul to the glorification of Thy goodness, and offer supplications and prayers unto Thy tenderness of heart, for our own sins and those of all Thy people, whom do Thou look upon in mercy, through the intercessions of the holy Theotokos.

Help us, save us, have mercy on us, raise us up, and keep us, O God, by Thy grace.

Choir   Lord, have mercy

Priest   Commemorating our most holy, most pure, most blessed and glorious Lady Theotokos and Ever-virgin Mary, with all the saints, let us commend ourselves and each other, and all our life unto Christ our God.

Choir   To Thee, O Lord

Priest   For Thou art the repose of our souls and bodies, and to Thee do we send up glory, to the Father, and to the Son, and to the Holy Spirit, now and ever, and unto ages of ages.

Choir   Amen

The Evening Litany

Priest   Let us complete our evening prayer unto the Lord.

Choir   Lord, have mercy

Priest   Help us, save us, have mercy on us, and keep us, O God, by Thy grace.

Choir   Lord, have mercy

Priest   That the whole evening may be perfect, holy, peaceful and sinless, let us ask of the Lord

Choir   Grant it, O Lord

Priest   An angel of peace, a faithful guide, a guardian of our souls and bodies, let us ask of the Lord.

Pardon and remission of our sins and transgressions, let us ask of the Lord.

All things that are good and profitable for our souls, and peace for the world, let us ask of the Lord.

That we may complete the remaining time of our life in peace and repentance, let us ask of the Lord

A Christian ending to our life; painless, blameless, and peaceful; and a good defense before the dread judgment seat of Christ, let us ask of the Lord.

Commemorating our most holy, most pure, most blessed and glorious Lady Theotokos and ever-virgin Mary, with all the saints, let us commend ourselves and each other, and all our life unto Christ our God.

Choir To Thee, O Lord

Priest For Thou art a good God and lovest mankind, and
unto Thee we ascribe glory; to the Father, and to the
Son, and to the Holy Spirit, now and ever, and unto
ages of ages

Choir Amen

Priest Peace be unto all.

Choir And to your spirit

Priest Let us bow our heads unto the Lord

Choir To Thee, O Lord

Priest O Lord our God, who didst bow the heavens and
come down for the salvation of mankind: Look upon
Thy servants and Thine inheritance; for unto Thee,
the awesome Judge, who lovest mankind, have Thy
servants bowed their heads, and submissively
inclined their necks, awaiting not help from men, but
asking Thy mercy, and looking confidently for Thy
salvation Guard them at all times, both during this
present evening and in the approaching night, from
every foe, from all adverse powers of the Devil, from
vain thoughts and from evil imaginations. Blessed
and glorified be the majesty of Thy kingdom: of the
Father, and of the Son, and of the Holy Spirit: now
and ever, and unto ages of ages.

Choir   Amen

The Aposticha

Choir   (Tone 3) Now the tongues have become a sign to all! for the Jews, Christ's ancestors in the flesh were faithless. Fallen from Divine grace, we fo the Gentiles have been granted the Divine Light. We have been strengthened by the diciples' words proclaiming the glory of the God of all. With them let us bend our hearts with our knees. Let us worship the Holy Spirit in faith, being confirmed by the Savior of our souls.

Reader   *Create in me a clean heart, O God, and renew a right spirit within me.*

Choir   Now the comforting Spirit has been poured out over all flesh. Beginning with the choir of the Apostles, He has spread His grace, communicating it to all the faithful. He gives proof of His mighty descent by distributing the fiery tongues, to the disciples, for the praise and glory of God. So now that our hearts have been spiritually enlightened, dtrengthened in faith by the Holy Spirit, let us pray that our souls may be saved.

Reader   *Cast me not away from Thy face and take not Thy Holy Spirit from me.*

Choir   Now the apostles are clothed with the power of Christ from on high, for the Comforter renews them.

He is renewed in them by a mystical newness of understanding. They preach to us in strange and exalted voices, teaching us to worship the eternal yet simple nature, the Tri-Personal nature of our Benefactor, the God of All! So being enlightened by their teaching, let us worship the Father with the Son and the Spirit, praying that our souls may be saved.

Reader *Glory to the Father, and to the Son, and to the Holy Spirit, now and ever, and unto ages of ages. Amen.*

Choir Come, let us worship the Tri-Personal Godhead, the Son in the Father with the Holy Spirit, the Father timelessly begets the co- reigning and co-etemal Son. The Holy Spirit was in the Father, glorified equally with the Son, One Power, One Substance, One Godhead! In worshipping Him, let us all say: Holy God: who made all things through the Son, with the cooperation of the Spirit. Holy Mighty: through whom we know the Father, through whom the Holy Spirit came into the world! Holy Immortal: the comforting Spirit, proceeding from the Father and resting in the Son. O Holy Trinity: glory to Thee!

St. Simeon's Prayer

Choir or Reader Lord, now lettest Thou Thy servant depart in peace, according to Thy word. For mine eyes have seen Thy salvation, which Thou hast prepared before the face of all people: a light to enlighten the Gentiles, and to be the glory of Thy people, Israel.

Reader Holy God, Holy Mighty, Holy Immortal, have mercy on us (3x)

Glory to the Father and to the Son and to the Holy Spirit, now and ever and unto ages of ages. Amen.

Most Holy Trinity have mercy on us, Lord cleanse us from our sins, Master pardon our transgressions, Holy One, visit and heal our infirmities for Thy Name's sake.

Lord have mercy, Lord have mercy, Lord have mercy.

Glory to the Father and to the Son and to the Holy Spirit, now and ever and unto ages of ages. Amen.

Our Father, who art in heaven, hallowed be Thy name. Thy kingdom come, Thy will be done on earth as it is in heaven. Give us this day our daily bread and forgive us our trespasses as we forgive those who trespass against us. And lead us not into temptation but deliver us from evil.

Priest For Thine is the Kingdom, and the power and the glory, now and ever and unto ages of ages.

Choir Amen

The Troparion (Tone 8)

The choir sings the troparion three times

Blessed art Thou, O Christ our God who hast revealed the fisherman as most wise by sending down upon them the Holy Spirit: through them Thou didst draw the world into Thy net. O Lover of man, glory to Thee.

The Dismissal

Priest Wisdom

Choir Father, bless.

Priest Christ our God, the Existing One, is blessed always, now and ever, and unto ages of ages.

Choir Amen. Preserve, O God, the Holy Orthodox Faith and Orthodox Christians, unto ages of ages.

Priest Most Holy Theotokos, save us!

Choir More honorable than the Cherubim, and more glorious beyond compare than the Seraphim: without defilement you gave birth to God the Word. True Theotokos, we magnify you!

Priest Glory to Thee, O Christ, our God, and our hope, glory to Thee!

Choir   Glory to the Father, and to the Son, and to the Holy Spirit, now and ever, and unto ages of ages. Amen. Lord, have mercy. (3) Father, bless.

Priest   May He who did empty Himself from the Paternal and Divine Bosom, and came down from heaven upon the earth, and took upon Himself all our nature, and made it divine, and after these things, again ascended into heaven and sitteth at the right hand of God the Father, and did send down the divine and holy Spirit, one in essence, equal in power, and equal in glory, and ever-existing with Him, up- on His holy Disciples and Apostles, and through Him did enlighten them, and through them the whole world, Christ our true God, through the intercessions of His all-immaculate and all- blameless holy Mother, of the holy, glorious, all laudable Preachers of God, the Spirit-bearing Apostles, and of all the Saints, have mercy on us and save us, for He is good and loveth man.

Choir   Amen